REAL

The Man and The Miracle

To order additional copies of this book, contact:
Xlibris
1-888-795-4274
www.Xlibris.com
Orders@Xlibris.com

ISBN: Softcover   978-1-9845-8409-0
       Hardcover   978-1-9845-8408-3
       EBook   978-1-9845-8407-6

Library of Congress Control Number: 2020911059

Print information available on the last page

Rev. date: 06/24/2020

REAL

The Man and The Miracle

BRITTNEY FLOWERS

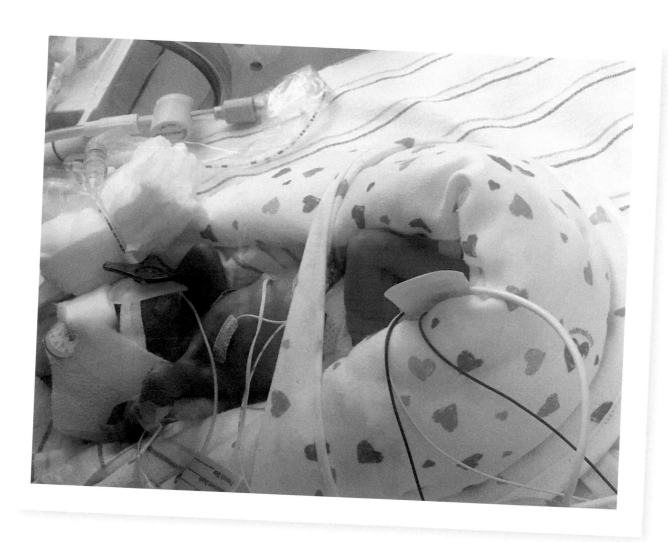

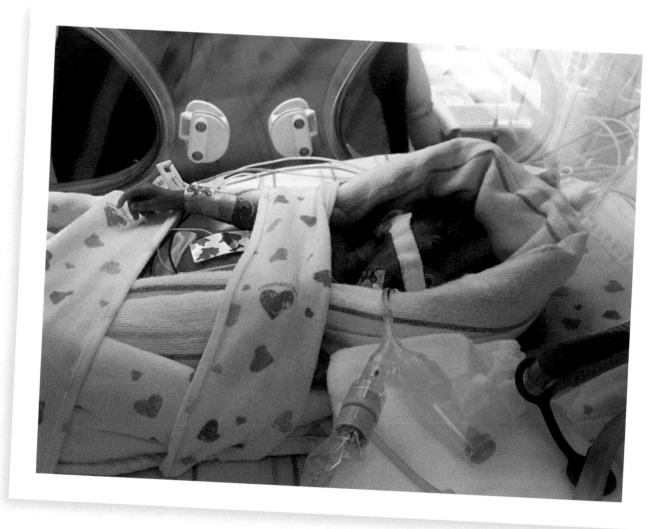

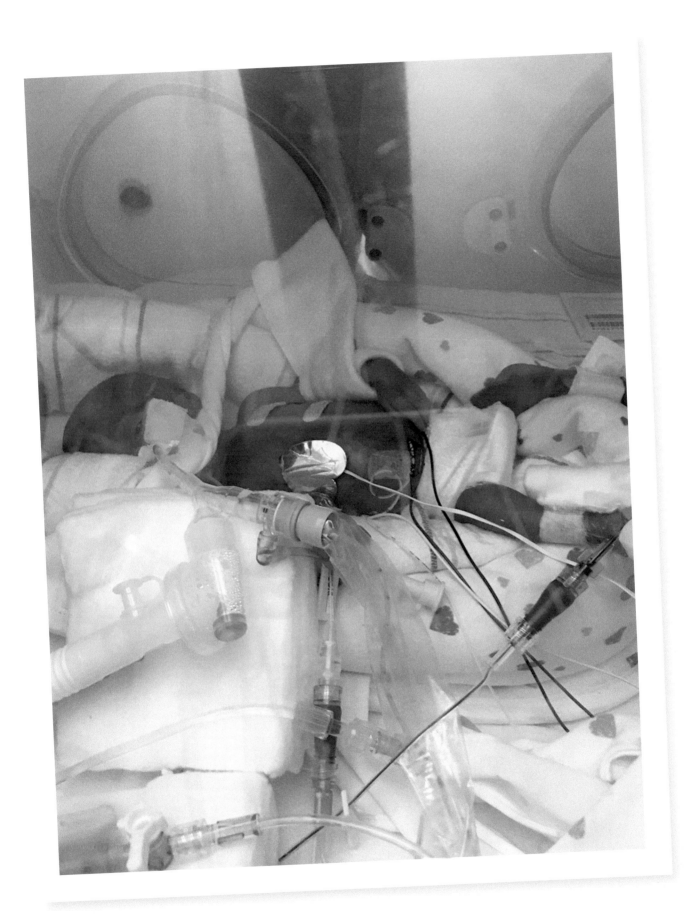

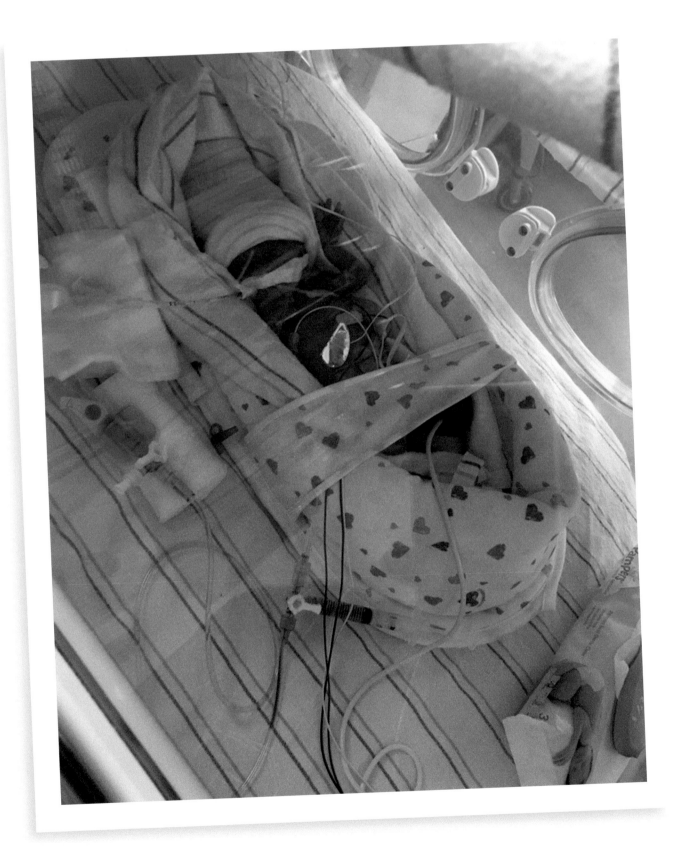

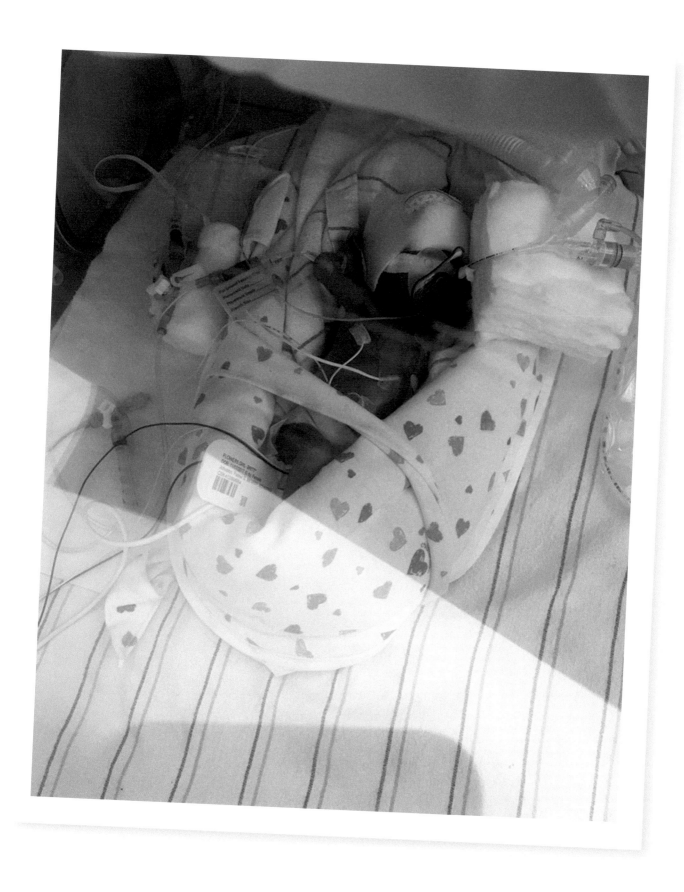

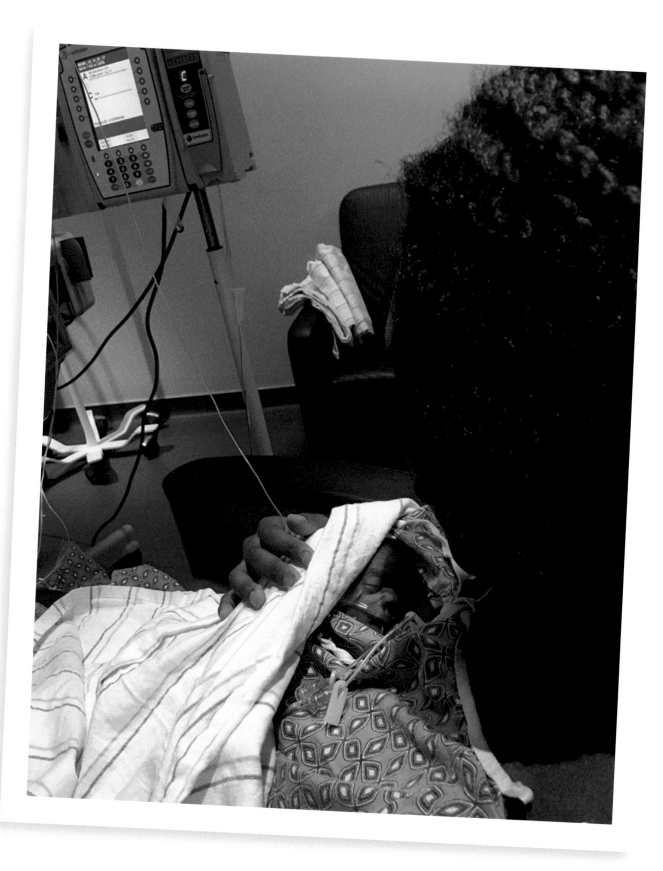

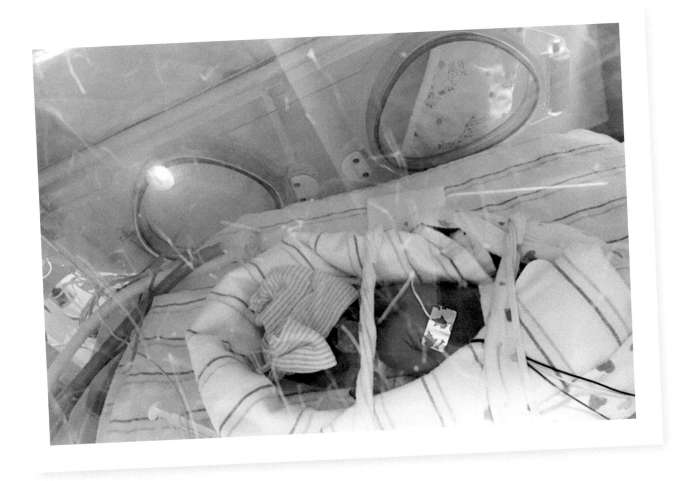

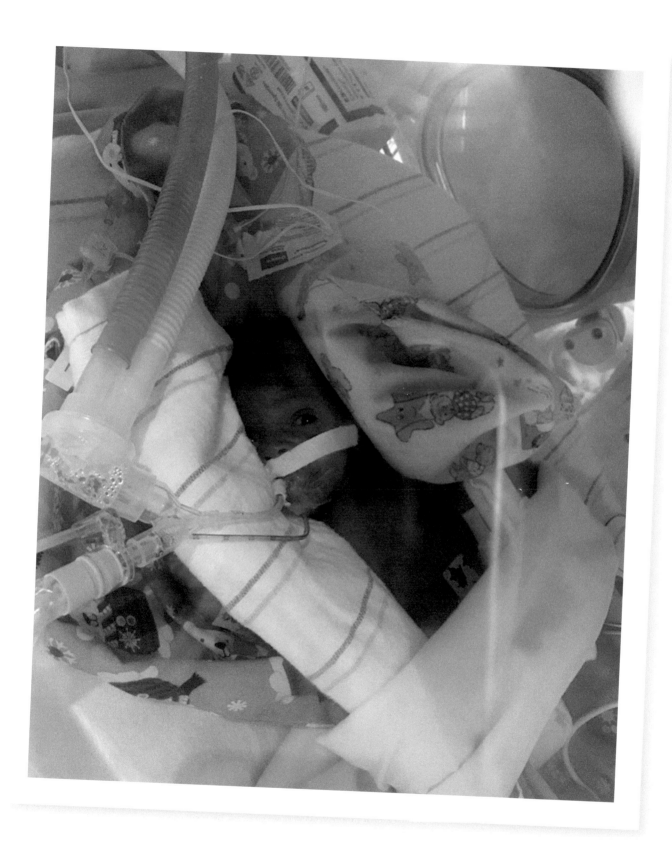

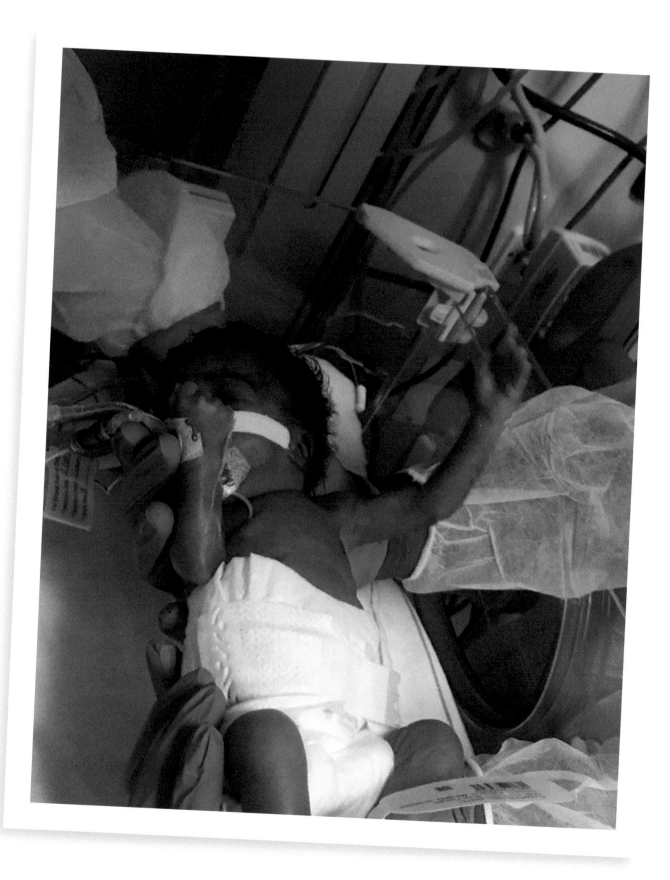

When women become pregnant; we all want a nice, happy, and healthy pregnancy. Some people get that, "while others" don't. When we first get pregnant, our thoughts get complicated. We think about wanting to get a abortion, was our decision wise, how scary it will be to tell somebody (including the child's father) and can we be truly be happy? We make every decision based on emotion. Our final thought is realizing we are being blessed by God. My mother raised me in church. Both sides mother and father side are christian. You don't have to be in church to give God time. I gave him time but do I give him what he wants? I have faith but do I really have faith or just saying it? I believe in God I'm just a young living life. The year of 2017 was my year of saving up for a car and finding a place. My problems were shopping, buying food and helping other people. I had to cut back on those things because I really was ready to have my own. I'm spoiled therefore I never thought about moving out at an early age plus my mother wasn't the type to push her children out. But as I was getting older I was ready to be on my own. I actually was doing really good staying focused.

Did I forget about God? Everytime I have my mind set on something, it never goes as planned. I was disappointed in myself. I wonder how come things don't ever go right with me. Did you put God first in everything you? I know God is real and he is right by my side. I told a few people what I had planned but it was people who I trusted. Sooner later I started talking to God and let him lead me in the right direction. I don't care what people think of me, just because they got it first doesn't mean I'm not going get it. I stayed pushing and remained focused. I looked as if I put God first. Am I going to get what I want quicker? No still had to wait. Few people told don't beat myself down about things, God time not always our time. I remained humble, kept working hard because in due time I was going to have what I was asking for. I'm a independent person, I got that from my mother. My boyfriend was right by my side.

My boyfriend and I were together for years. Our life is good just enjoying each other trying to get our stuff together. We both were on the same page. He was staying with his sister and I was living with my granddaddy. But I mainly stayed at his sister's house. Every relationship is not perfect but if you both want it will work it out. I had my days one foot out the door, I could only take so much. It's not all about cheating, sometimes womens don't feel love or wanting and don't have that communication. But through it all we got back right. I got his back and he got my front. A man can treat you so good but make stupid decisions. The decisions they make can also have a woman leave. He made sure I was straight at all times. My family likes him and of course his family likes me. He told me one day, baby I'm happy I found you. Every woman brings something out in a man. Whatever I did, I love him for showing he wanted me here. One summer family came down for the summer, therefore it was outing times. I love my family so much it's nothing but fun and happiness. Summer is my favorite season, birthdays, cookouts, trips and kids out of school.

You can do lots of stuff over the summer. I was ready to get off to enjoy my family. It's just hot and I feel light headed if I stay in the heat so long. That heat know joke at all. My aunties always tell me to drink water but I'll drink juice. We had a gathering at my granddaddy house for my family that came down. It was so hot outside I felt like I was about to pass out. I had a bottle of water and it felt so good my body needed it. On July 4, 2017 my sister who was turning 19 years old still couldn't drink. LOL. We went to my cousin's house. We were drinking, laughing and just having a good time with the family. After the cookout we tried to decide was we were going downtown or the movies. Nobody didn't know what they wanted to do. We were tired from the cookout. We just went to my other cousin's house and stayed there for hours. I had family from Atlanta, Maryland and Oklahoma.

The cousins had their outing as the parents. We all went out together some but the adults can't hang too long with the youngest. On their last day we all went to the beach and enjoyed ourselves. I hate when they leave, I wish everyone stayed closer. A couple of weeks after I started feeling light headed again, here Metri now fussed at me not drinking water. The feel will come and go therefore I took some medicine. I hated getting sick. All I do is sleep but I work so much that's why I am tired. My best friend called me one day. I can't say I'm tired or hungry around her because the first thing that comes to her mind is, You Pregnant! I always say girl know babies come out of me. Metri and I are just laughing. My 22nd birthday in August I really enjoyed myself. One day I was off work but Metri was at work. That feeling came back again. I texted him I was going to the emergency room. I hate the emergency room but I really had to see what's going on. My body felt weak and drained.

When I got there I waited for 30 minutes until they called me in the back. They took blood work and got some urine from me. Come to find out I was dehydrated, I got a IV in me to put some fluid in me. I was there for three hours. Metri checked on me and I told him everything was good and what was wrong. He replied baby, you got to start drinking more water, like I didn't already know that. While I'm laying on the bed getting some rest the nurse came in and asked if was I okay? I said yes. The nurse said after I'm done I can leave, 10 minutes later another nurse came in to inform me that I was 7 weeks pregnant. I woke up all the way. I'm thinking to myself what in the world I have been drinking and stuff. Before I even told Metri he went to text me saying, baby I'm in the back of the police car. I called him so fast he didn't answer so I texted he took a minute to reply. Then going text back I'm playing baby, Had me work up, it wasn't the right time for playing.

When the nurse told me I was pregnant, I was sad and happy. I thought this was a stepping stone towards my independence. Eventually being on my own and financially stable. This was kind of a two step back for me. I got to take things easy. I told my childs father along with a few close friends and family. He was so happy he was calling and texting getting on my nerves. He will say I knew it and start laughing. This is not my first pregnancy which everybody thought. The first time I gotten pregnant; I had a miscarriage due to the baby stopped growing inside the womb.

The second time I didn't know the cause of it really but Metri said the cord was wrapped around the baby. This my third pregnancy I had know idea how this was going to turn out. He was happy every time and he never left my side. That's my longtime partner with or without his child. He never changed on me and didn't feel any type of way against me. During my two miscarriage he were right there. I truly love him for not leaving, not one but two of his kids didn't make it. We are not perfect at all but it's the things he shows me that make me hang on to him. But I still know my worth. You have low down mens out here will actually leave their girl. But I got a good one. There are several different levels of pregnancy, unfortunately mines were high risk. I had to go to the memorial provident building due to my high risk. I went to one obgyn but once I lost my first child I had to go to memorial hospital. As my high risk is scary for me. I lost two kids if I lost this one it's just not meant to be. I blamed myself at first but then sometimes things not meant to be at that moment. Then I realized down the line after I had healed from it. Things started to happen in my life with my job and I wasn't going to be able raise a child. My boyfriend had his issue going on as well. I was being extremely careful this time, while my boyfriend ensured I was well taken care of. It was our duty to make sure our baby was safe. We couldn't bare another miscarriage. I had a big support system. You can cause high risk if you have high blood pressure, depression, health problems, smoking and any other things that can harm your pregnancy. As I look up the age of 17 or younger and 35 or older could be considered high risk. I never had to worry about being disrespected, never stressed, never worried about what he was doing behind my back and in this generation females are messy and it would've been known. You will never see one without seeing the other, we are like love bugs stuck together Sometimes the cause of being stressed can be how the mother is going to do this. Mother's want to give our child/children the world. I know I do, when I got depressed it was only because I'm trying to get in my own place and I want myself together. Having a child is a job that you can't quit. We go through body changes just don't be feeling yourself like that. Now that I was pregnant I can't do a lot. I used to cry out the blue for some reason because of my emotional use to get to me. Doctors appointment twice a week just to make sure the baby was good inside. Everything was looking good. Later down the line I got a text from one of my cousins Elexis, she was pregnant as well.

My cousin and I are so close, we did everything together. Now that we have grown and in relationships we barely hang. But when we do get together nothing changes. We were happy for each and checked on each other every other day or so. Our kids are going to be just like we are. Cousin but more like sisters. What's crazy because when I got pregnany the second time she were pregnant and we both had a miscarriage. It was crazy how we both went through the same thing. I didn't want the world or the rest of my family know yet. My plan was go to get a place than tell them. When I started showing a little I couldn't hide it from my family anymore but the world I did. I started showing when I was 3 to 4 months old. I was a working young lady and wasn't gonna stop but sooner than later I had to slow down. I was working so much to the point my feet got big but my manager had me sitting in the office to rest. I had eaten a whole pizza that I shouldn't have had and my face had puffed up badly.

All this swollen off and on it was all a part of pregnancy. I went to my cousin Elexis house one day after work. My aunt saw me. She told my cousin and I we needed to slow down. We were going too much while we were pregnant. My goal was to have my place and I was pushing towards it, saving and all. I got up one morning for work, I went to the restroom and my face was swollen. I got big overnight. I went to work while my co-worker was walking out. She stopped and said, "BRITTNEY WHAT WRONG WITH YOUR FACE?" I replied, I'm pregnant am I? She said no you shouldn't be that big like something is wrong. It went down through the day but my feet got swollen. I had to take off my shoes. I was doing good until about 22 weeks ago. My feet had gotten swollen, along with my face and arms. Another morning I woke up swollen from head to toe. I'm still thinking it was just because of pregnancy, but I know I needed to go to the doctor. The doctor told me to keep my feet propped up and get some rest. I did just what he said so I didn't have to be put on bed rest. It was helping a little. I was ready to find out what I was having, I wanted to have a girl. I was praying for a girl. It didn't matter to Metri what we were having. He just knows if it's a boy it's gonna be a Jr. and if it's a girl he thought the name was going to be Demetrica. But I already had a girl name in mind and I had that since I was in 3rd or 4th grade. I took it from a girl in my class and I told myself if I have a little girl that's going to be her name. We actually was going back and forth with the girl's name. He wanted to keep it going with him and his sister's name. But the baby going already has his last name therefore I was going to name the baby if it's a girl. If we have another girl in the future, he could name her because I already had a name in mind. He finally let the name go and let me name the girl. My sister went with me to the doctor to find out what I was having, I didn't want to know. I wasn't sure if I wanted to have a reveal or not. It was my birthday and we just did a little something, it wasn't really big.

Due to me not really sitting down actually not planning it I didn't let nobody know. But we're having our baby girl! I was so excited I got a mini growing inside of me. We are about to work daddy nerves. After I found out what I was having I started going shopping. I'm having a Girl! It was going into tornado season of course we had to evacuate. My family and I went to my aunt's house in Atlanta. Metri stayed and I was upset because why will he stay? I was calling his phone know answer due to the lights going out. Couldn't charge his phone and turned around. I left my card and everything back home. I was just over everything. But we all made a way out of it. On the way back home, still trying to get in touch with Metri, I called his sister to see if she talked to him and a few more people. Nobody talked to him, at this point I'm mad and worried if he is good. When he finally called I felt so much better. When we got back home I got some rest and relaxed.

On November 10, 2017, I went to my appointment for an infusion. My mom left me there and 5 minutes later, she had to turn back around to come get me. Unfortunately, I couldn't get it, but due to my blood pressure being so high; I had to rush to the emergency room. I have never known having high blood pressure. On my way there I'm praying that my blood pressure will be down and I can go home. Metri was in the car with me at the time, he made sure I was checked in but he couldn't stay because he had an interview. When I arrived, my pressure was checked. It was still high. I had to stay overnight. After several tests, the doctor diagnosed me with preeclampsia. What is preeclampsia? "How can it affect my baby and I?" I questioned." "It's a disorder in pregnancy with a side effect being high blood pressure, protein in urine, and swelling of the body", replied the doctor. I wish they had caught it earlier, but nobody knew. I was 26 weeks and they were trying to hold me until the 27th but it depended on the baby reaction. They put me into a room where I will be until the baby comes. I wanted to bust out crying. Why is this happening? What is going on? I want to have a regular pregnancy. The holidays are coming up, am I going to be here? Lord why? I can't question God, what am I doing? Just why me? What am I doing wrong? As I lay down while the nurses, putting IV in my arm, putting a DVT (Deep Vein Thrombosis) pump on my leg for I don't have blood clots and monitor on my stomach to hear the baby heart beat also to see what the baby is doing. While they were doing that I just remember my mother always told me to give God sometimes because one day he's gonna get it one way or the other. I might not like it but I'm not going to have any choice but to reach out to him. I was fighting my tears until I got alone. Everything I had planned was ruined. Day two in here I started not to let in bother me. I received several ultrasounds a day to check on the baby's condition and to see if the placenta was getting blood. She had her moments. It wasn't looking good but I prayed and prayed, the baby was going head down. I might have this baby any moment. I just wanted my baby to be okay. I didn't plan on being here, I thought they were going to do a check up and release me. "Only God knows," I said. He will not put more on me than I can bear". The doctor and his assistants checked on me everyday. I thought everything was getting better, except my blood pressure, but I had medication for that. The assistant checked my breathing. She asked me, Am I Okay? I said yes. She replied Are You Sure? You wouldn't Lie To Me? I told her I'm good, nothing wrong with me. After several checks from her and the others, she reported to me that she heard a crackling sound. Every time the assistant spoke something negative; I spoke something positive. Two nurses checked on me periodically and encouraged me.

Clearly the assistant had people thinking I was sick but I was really good. Tried not to let that bother me, I'm worried more about my child. The doctor talked about my baby. Due to my conditions, I would have my baby earlier and she would be placed in the Neonatal Intensive Care Unit (NICU). I was having a premature baby. In this situation my child will be needing lots of therapy to get her on the right path. I took it as my baby going to be kind of special aid. I wanted to burst out in tears. This wasn't posted to be like this. I wanted to have a normal pregnancy. I keep saying to myself why me? Why Me? Why me? This my third pregnancy and it's heartbreaking. I wanted to just everything over with. I informed my boyfriend the news, but I could see the pain in his eyes. He was so worried he didn't even smoke as much. His #1 girl was his only concern. I waited for an alone moment to talk to Jesus. He had all the answers. We have been through enough. My mom or Metri stayed with me. I used to wake Metri up because I was in my feelings. He told me don't worry God got us. All we wanted was a healthy baby and that was my prayer.

My due date was February 22, 2018, but I expected her to come before then. I did not want to be here doing the holidays but the longer she holds on the better it will be. One night after my company left I was eating fruit and my body started to feel strange. My mom had gone home to get some clothes therefore I couldn't wait until she came back. I called my nurse immediately. She checked on me, gave me some medicine, and monitored me for a while. I had a machine attached to my body to monitor my baby's heartbeat. That was the most angelic sound to hear. I had to use the restroom. As the nurses assisted me to the restroom, I fainted!!!! As the nurses rushed me back into the bed. They called for help. I didn't know what was going on. I could hear the assistant calling me, but I couldn't respond. I felt someone hitting me, but I couldn't respond. A response finally sprouted out. I remember someone asking, "who to call?" "My mama!", I exclaimed. I went back out. I could feel myself being transported somewhere. I can feel a cutting happening, but I couldn't respond or resist. I thought I was dreaming, but an emergency was taking place. I can hear the voice of my mother and aunt. It was calming, but I couldn't respond still.

On November 17, 2017 at 2:04am. I birthed a baby girl. Ca'layia Aubrii Tremble. 1 pound and 7 ounces. When I returned to myself, I turned my head to the left and right; all I saw was my auntie. My body begins to get cold. My nurse was coming in right on time. She went to get me a warm blanket and wrapped me in it. I laid there thinking to myself, what happened? What's going on? I was told I had fluid in my lungs this whole time being in the hospital. I was praying for my baby, but it was me who needed it as well. I was sick this whole time any symptoms; I could've lost my life. The staff was aware, but I felt normal. I thanked God for getting me through it. Now the Preeclampsia is more serious than I realized. You usually get preeclampsia when you get clothes to your due date but I got it early. Ca'layia was transported to NICU getting situated, while her mom was recovering. All I could think is "where is her father?" All I saw was my aunt. After being rotated and comforted, she informed me he was with our daughter. I was jealous he saw her first and I couldn't yet. I later found out I had multiple aunts, cousins and sister present at the birth of Ca'layia, but I didn't remember because I was out of it. As other visitors came to see her, Metri took them to see her. I began to become angered; I was ready to see my baby. When time came for me to see her, I became nervous. I was afraid of what she would look like; due to her being preemie. Metri escorted me to her. I was excited and nervous at the same time. I finally saw my daughter!!! I wanted to cry. I hated to see her in such a state. Seeing her lay there with so many tubes attached to her, numerous machines all beeping, her eyes closed, I-V connected to her feet and arms and bloodlines running.

My baby was fighting for her life. It became unbearable for a minute, but the mother in me stood tall and allowed me to endure. We went back to the room to get some rest. When I rose, I saw that Metri had gone to check on our angel. I begin to pray and ask God for a speedy recovery. I have a family now and I needed God to keep us that way. The next day I had a full house of visitors. My best friend, mother, sister, kids, sister's boyfriend, and numerous others. I had so many visitors come in, the nurse said; "you are truly loved". I was encouraged. They spend the entire day with me. They brought much laughter and joy into the room. It was for me to go home, but my baby had to stay. I was so heartbroken.

I was supposed to leave with my entire family, not with just Metri and I. I went to see my baby before I left, while taking it easy on myself. My first day home and my baby aren't with me. I missed my baby! I couldn't get up and leave to go see her until I was completely healed. I had many sleepless nights, crying, praying, and thinking. I was never so depressed in life but this was a scary journey. My biggest fear was getting a call my daughter didn't make. I would have lost it, my life would've been over with life. Doing this time I was really second guessing on everything. I was scared to lose my child. I couldn't imagine my life without her. I have been through alot to lose a child. I wasn't sure if God was hearing me. Everyone kept saying keep the faith. Thanksgiving came around; everyone came over and enjoyed family time, but I couldn't bear the fact that my baby wasn't here with me. I got up and went to the restroom. I began to cry, but I couldn't allow everyone to see, so I washed my face. It was hard keeping faith: I was scared something was going to happen to her. My niece helped relieve my mind of all negative thoughts. She kept a smile on my face, alongside my family and Metri. Due to the weather I didn't get a chance to go see her at the hospital, but we called and checked on her. The next day we went to see her. Everything seemed normal besides her eyes being protected. We couldn't hold her yet due to weight and some of her conditions, all I could do is admise her little body moving and her tiny mouth. I know my baby was in pain; but I couldn't hear her cry. She had to have a couple of blood transfusions. They inserted a UVC/UAC to have them operate at different times.

They inserted a tube up her nose and throat to help her breathe. She had gotten two peripherally central catheters that connected tubes from her veins to veins near her heart. She received a lumbar puncture, which inserted a needle for them to receive fluids. It was very overwhelming watching her receive all this treatment. Thanks be to God, because they all came back good. I knew my baby was a fighter. She had no reaction during the process. I wanted to take the stress off her so bad. I was full of emotions, stressful, sad, scared, guilty, mad, loving, and happy all at the same time. I wanted my daughter home immediately; I was fully frustrated. With them having performing procedures on my little angel. I was starting to be heart broken, but about two weeks my baby started doing a little better. Later down the line they took her off the ventilator very slowly; as nervous I was for her not breathing fully on her own and her lungs not fully being fully ready. She responded very well to that process, but her oxygen levels were scared, so of course they placed her on oxygen. Ca'Layia was diagnosed with Respiratory Distress Syndrome, Pulmonary Insufficiency Immaturity, Bronchopulmonary Dysphasic, Apnea, and Thrombocytopenia. She was at risk for Intraventricular Hemorrhage & developmental delay, Oliguria, Adrenal Insufficiency, immure retina, a retinopathy of prematurity. After such overwhelming issues, all I could do was pray. Yet she continued to fight. I begin to question my baby's life after that.

Furthermore, her lungs were extremely weak, she had a hold near her heart that caused a lack of blood cells, skin infection, and major respiratory diseases. To top all that off, my biggest scare was her blood vessels in her brain not fully developed. Being that she is a preemie, everything wasn't going to come along slower than normal. The doctors instructed me that breast feeding would get her stronger. The pressure came on me heavy because I felt like I was not pumping enough for my little fighter. The nurse encouraged me continuously. I believe my other biggest fear was my child being special needs or having a disability. I thought to myself "it's nothing wrong with that, but I knew that I would have to love a little harder to ensure a normal life. I would have to quit my job and ensure my child was well taken care of. Only God has the last word from here. I had major faith in Him and tried my hardest not to worry. Sunday, December 17, 2017 it was her dad's birthday. Early that morning I received a phone call to come to hospital immediately.

When I arrived, I was informed that her oxygen level dropped tremendously and she had to return to the ventilator, I was so nervous I began to shake. Today made one month for my baby. Later her dad arrived, I knew he didn't want to hear the news but endured and still enjoyed his day. I was so focused on my child, nothing else mattered at that moment. They asked me to sign for some pictures, but I didn't care; I just wanted her tube out by then. I prayed and prayed that her whole respiratory would increase for the better. Christmas Day arrived. I wanted my baby home. I hoped for a Christmas miracle. Today they took pictures. I didn't want them because my baby still had tubes, but I kept them for memories. After knowing she was well, I went home to have family time. As I constantly checked on her. She did very well all day. I felt so depressed, but I knew I had to trust the Lord. For the next few days, I begin to pray every few minutes. I felt like he wasn't hearing me. I knew don't pray and worry, so I had to get myself together. After I started worrying, everything started looking better. She started to gain weight, she didn't have any more procedures, blood count was great, brain was healthy, feeding was going well. I was thanking God. I knew my baby was going to be healthy, and I didn't have to worry about disability. All tests came back good. The devil tried to knock me off track. Couple of weeks later Lay had a little problem with her stomach and kept her food down.

They took her off food for 24 hours to see if everything would subside. My baby was hungry, but all she could do was move her mouth. It didn't work. They stopped giving fluids and gave her medicine to flush her out. That worked little by little. All I could think about getting that tube out so I held her. New Year's came and left, but I saw God moving more and more. By the first week of the new year, we were able to hold, wash, cloth, bath, and change her. It seemed that she only poo-poo on me, but I didn't mind. Do it with your daddy some. She was making progress. This process thus far has really encouraged my heart and strengthened my faith in God. I felt stronger and wiser. I was able to trust him more and faith was stronger than ever. I hope to have her home by the end of the month. When I asked the nurse, she was unsure due to her respiratory. I didn't mind being patient because I wanted her to be as healthy as possible coming home. Towards the end of January she started having problems with acid reflux. Once again, they stopped her feeding and ran some tests. I tried my hardest not to let it discourage me. I just prayed. It seemed like every time I didn't pray or offer up thanks; something would tigger wrong.

I had to stop that devil I prayed and gave thanks to God, good or bad. I got shaken a little only when I wasn't sure what they were doing. The reflux was down and it will flare up again. They couldn't figure it out. In my opinion, they should've prepared her before meals. Rather they switched her position from her back to her side. It didn't change the outcome. The second week in February I received a phone call stating that she had to have surgery. Her acid reflux had gotten so bad it began to back up in her lungs. As I went to sign the papers. I see my daughter with an IV in her forehead. It was hard to find for them to find veins, being that she was a preemie. This was very hard to see as her mother. It was the day after Valentine's Day she had the surgery. I called every hour, but they kept saying she didn't return yet. I was trying to see what was taking so long. I was now getting upset. I later got a call from a doctor. I was greeted with "are you Ca'Layia Tremble mom?" His voice was so suspenseful I didn't know what to think.

"Surgery went well", he exclaimed. He informed me that they were going to start her on feeding again, with close monitoring. Once again, I birthed a fighter. Her nurses named her feisty. My sister went to see her. After I got off work, my mother and I went, but I couldn't bear to see my baby like that again. Days after things started to progress, her feeding was going well, and her breathing was increasing. They begin to feed her through a bottle. We were excited. She had days with her nurses and others with her parents. The overall goal was to get her to drink and eat at the same time. After a few days she progressed; well enough to leave the NICU. thank you, Jesus!! I was able to move my baby to a regular room. I didn't expect her to be moving with oxygen, but that didn't matter, she was getting better. We had to run it through her nose.

We had one foot out the door. We begin to unbox her car seat and prepare for a home arrival. She only had one oxygen episode but it self-regulated. I was able to lay next to her; she held my finger. This was the best feeling ever. She passed her car seat challenge. Everyday her oxygen level would drop a little, but our little fighter always fought it back to normal. I had to stay over to learn procedures to take her at home. I was able to have mother and daughter time. Her father checked on us, but I was so excited. It felt like we were home already. She slept great through the night. She only woke up to eat and be changed as any normal baby would. I prayed her lungs would be strong before we were released. The doctor came in the morning and asked how our nights were? After giving her the great report, she leased her to go home. God knew what was best for. She went home with oxygen, a monitor, and a machine for her gastrostomy tube (g-tube).

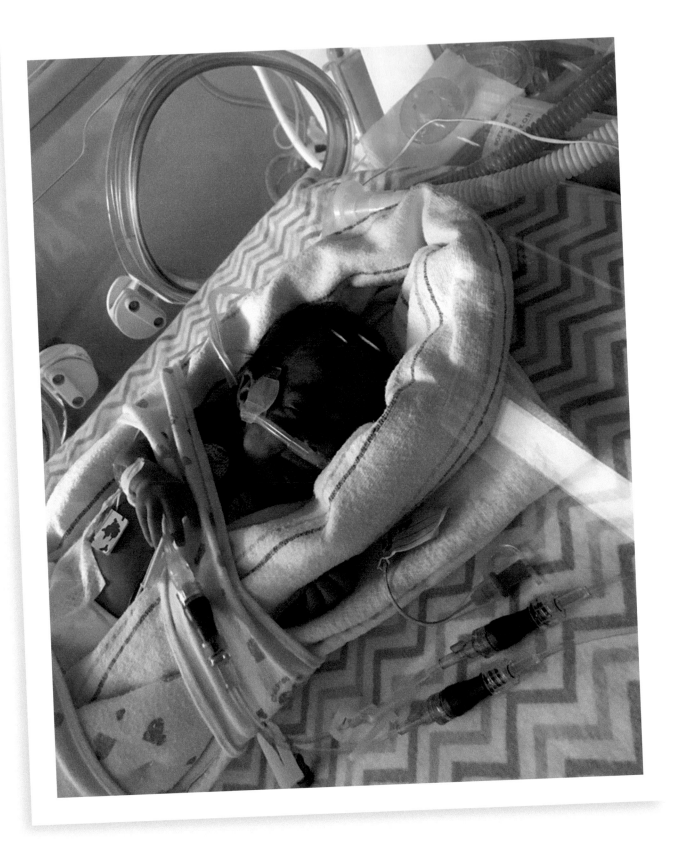

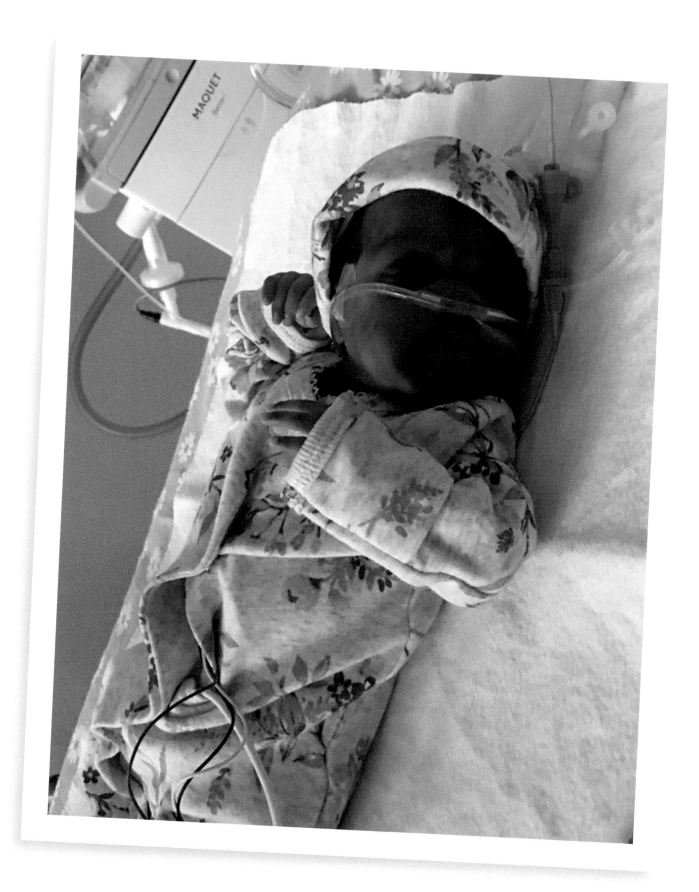

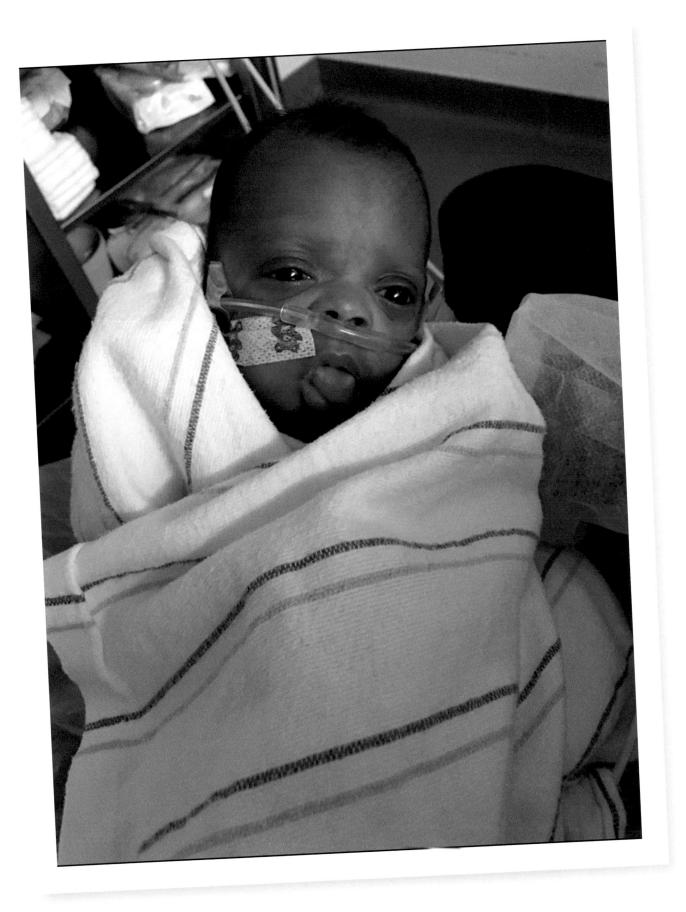

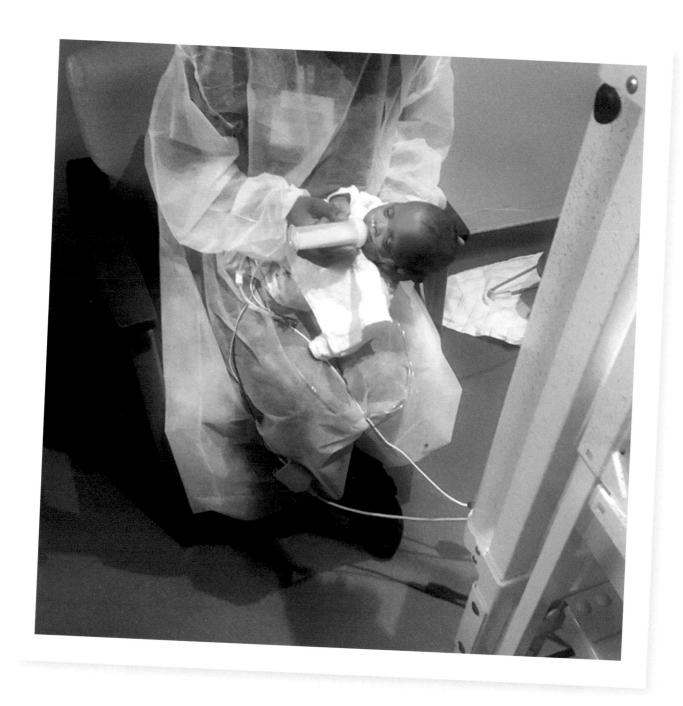

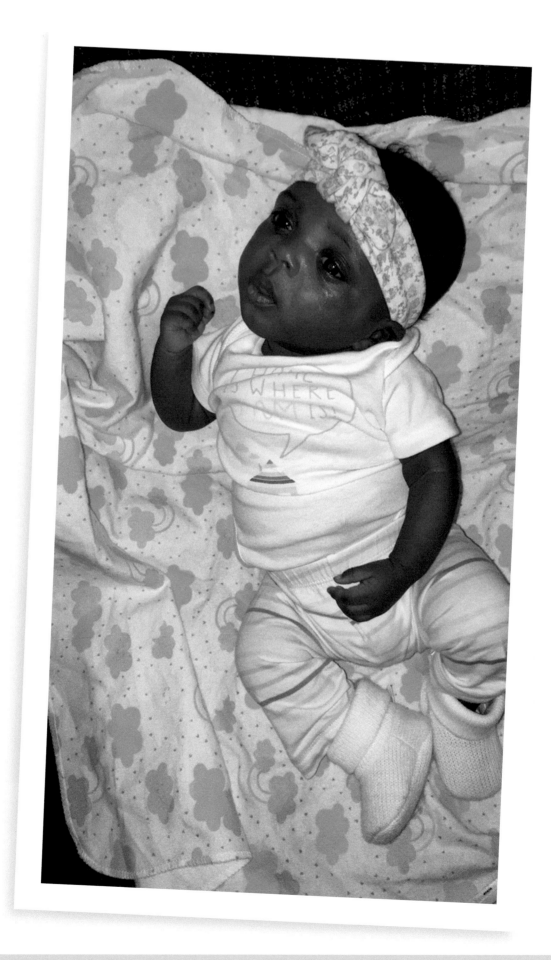

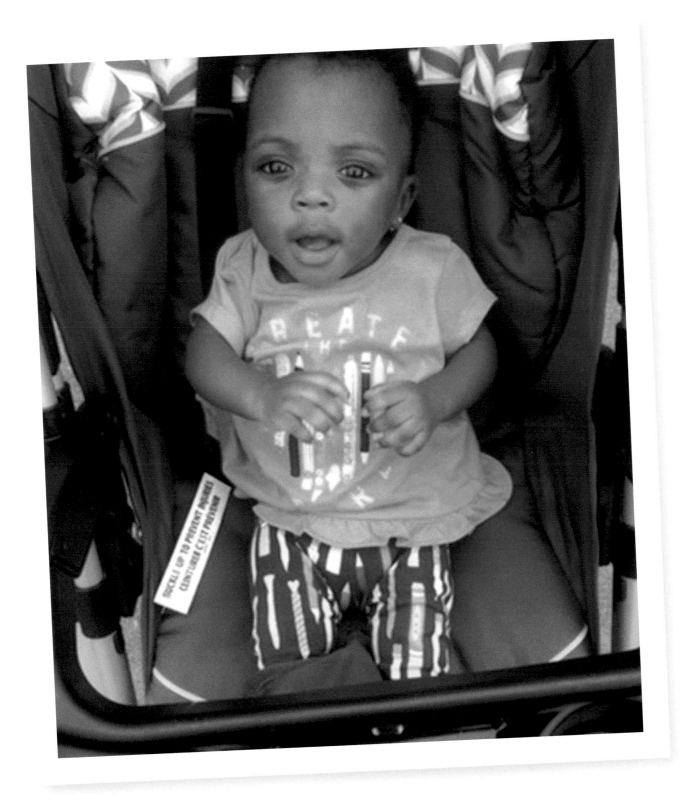

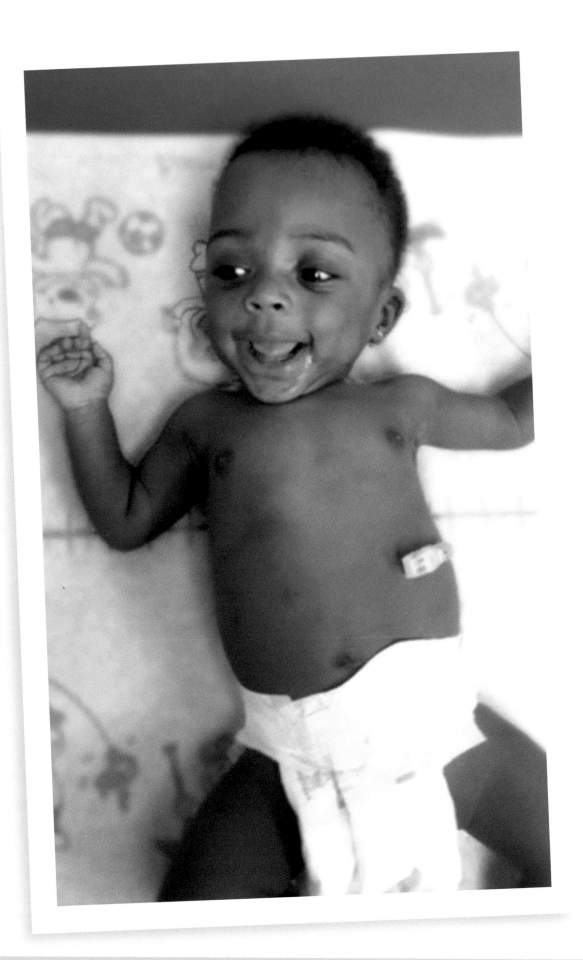

I prayed it didn't happen, but it was best for her. On March 28, 2018 our baby girl was going home. The best day of our life! First day home some of her cousins and aunties were waiting for her. Everybody came to see her. It didn't matter to me, but if you wanted to hold her; it was imperative they wash their hands. If you were a smoker who had just smoked, change your shirt and wash it again (her father mainly). I didn't care my child wasn't going back to the hospital. We had been there 104 days, and when we left, I said, "we won't be back." I did everything in my power to make sure Ca'Layia was in a safe environment. We agreed Lay wasn't going to go out until we both were ready. I took off work for a couple of months due to Lay issues. I know her father would've been good but he wasn't like me. He was more scared he was going to hurt her than me. Besides, her father and I were staying in different households at the time. We felt better because she stayed in the house for a while due to her lungs. Every morning he was right by our side.

Our little feisty baby had been through a lot. She didn't need any more problems. After being home a few days, everything seemed good. Nighttime her monitor was going off due to oxygen level decreasing. One morning we were laying down, I wrapped my arm around her, and I thought she stopped breathing. I said" Lay! Ca'Layia! I shock her a little. She finally started to move, so I gave her a kiss and attempted to return to bed. I was scared for my life. I thought my girl was gone. I was frightened. I laid my hands on her, and I prayed, I said, "God please keep her covered". I held her close by me every night. To make sure she was good. I thought to myself, "My daughter is finally home! I thank God everyday she made it.

Can you imagine taking your baby to the doctor appointments two times, or even three times a week? Caring Lay, rolling her big oxygen tank, carrying her monitor bag on my shoulder, carrying her g-tube on my back and her baby bag began to become very depressing when I had to go alone. People were looking at me crazy. I just wanted to turn back around and call it quits. It was hard for me to evaluate why her monitor was going off, while simultaneously observing why her g-tube was going off. The oxygen tank cord came off while I was walking. I had to stop to get everything together. Tears had dropped a couple of times. I just wanted this all to be over. But I wanted my child to be healthy. She is going to her gastroenterologist, pulmonologist and her primary doctor. Once again, I was scared. She was doing good at home, but when we got to the doctors it was a different story. She was on different types of medicines that she had to take once a day or twice a day. Full time mother and other responsibilities were very stressful. I cried every night wondering when this was going to be over. April 12, 2018 we had to rush her to the ER. She was having episodes with her oxygen dropping due to her reflux. I feared holding her but praying to God "keep my baby." When we finally got there, they took an e-ray and ran tests. She had to stay overnight. They needed to keep an eye on her. It saddens me we were back at Memorial Hospital after I said we weren't coming back. "Why is this happening to us again?" I prayed. "God is not done with us yet!", "we made it this far!" he isn't going let us down "I proclaimed and believed. I thought positive. I love my child and I don't know what I'll do with her. She slept good through the night and fept her food down. We went home later on the next day after a visit from her primary doctor. I still didn't get to rest. I was worried about her condition. We also had to visit her pulmonologist (Lungs) doctor. She turned her oxygen up and put her on Flovent. She had to take two puffs a day to get those lungs stronger. The last doctor visit was her gastroenterologist. She wasn't gaining the weight like she should. Therefore, they had to change her formula from neon-sure to elcare.

One night I woke up and Lay had pulled her oxygen off. It was under her neck, and I had known idea how long it was off. I took it from around her neck fast, checked on her, and left it off. The next day she went without her oxygen and she did good. I was listening to the doctors so much one day I thought to myself, you be her doctor some days. I am around her more than the doctors therefore I know how my child is. I started treating my daughter. I took her oxygen off to see how she would do. Once I saw her oxygen dropping one or two numbers, I put the tube back in. I kept doing it. She had gotten used to it. I still was giving her the two puffs. As time passed, I believe she didn't need it. I took it off her before the doctor instructed me to remove it from her. She slept with the tube in at night until she got adjusted to it.

Once again, we were off to the doctor again. Before I knew it, she was off the oxygen in May. We kept her on that regiment for a couple of days. Just as an experiment. May was a good month for us. Everything was working in our favor. I enjoyed my first Mother's Day with her. We celebrated her nana's birthday. That was no stress for her father and I conceived our miracle. Her acid reflux started acting up a couple of times every month. It was something Lay had gone through due to her preemie. Her weight and growth fluctuated. The doctors said she was taking time to get on the right path. She was gaining weight, but not as much as she should have. She is growing slowly, but I pray for her weight and growth to be together. In the month of June and October things started to get a little easier. She didn't have so many doctor's appointments. Her father's first Father's Day, our daughter was Christened. She was finally able to meet her father's side of the family. When we started going out more. Each outing we were seeing butterflies flying everywhere. Especially when we went outside on the porch. One day it was two outside flying around us. This meant something to me. I love my daughter with all my heart. I'm going to always stand by her side. I look at it as in the beginning she was a caterpillar who was fighting her way up to be free from the pain.

I later on went back to work. I was sad because I had to leave my baby for the very first. My cousin or aunt was watching her due to her having that g-tube in. I knew she was in good hands. Since the g-tube still in her father didn't want to watch he was literally scared and thought he was going to hurt her. Her birthday was coming up and I wanted to have her big party; due to me not having a baby shower or anything when she came home. I tried to contract everyone I knew. A good bit of people said they were coming. Unfortunately, my auntie had passed away a couple of days before her birthday; and we were having her funeral on Lay Birthday. I was very disappointed. On that Sunday, it was stressful. I was angry. I didn't plan how I wanted it and I just wanted to go home. Lay had gotten sick, and I didn't know how. We had to take her to the emergency room immediately after her gathering. She had gotten a bad cold and had been congested tremendously. We were there all night. Morning came, and I was glad it was over. She started to feel better.

Thanksgiving was coming up and I was happy because we got to spend our first Thanksgiving together as a family. Days before, we went back to the emergency room and they kept her this time. Knowing this the same time she was in the NICU. I didn't know what it was. Lay was getting sick so easy. I thought to myself "this was sad we are going through this again". We spent our time in the hospital for Thanksgiving. Again, Metri, Lay's father, told me to go home and he will stay with her. It still wasn't the same, we weren't together as an entire family. We took turns. She went home two days after. I didn't take her out of the house as much as we couldn't take it anymore. Thankfully, we had a good Christmas and New Year's.

In the beginning of 2019 everything was going well, Lay still had her G-Tube and everything seemed fine, but around February the G-Tube accidentally came out. We then rushed Lay to her doctor's office, since the G-Tube came out and it wasn't time, they had to clean everything and put the G-Tube back in. As my sister, mother, and I watched the doctor and nurse clean the G-Tube, Lay was crying and screaming while they were cleaning because the little hole that her G-Tube sits in was shooting out blood. Tears started falling from my sister and I eyes, because our girl was hurting. This all happened six months ago, but this time after the G-Tube accidentally slipped out they left it out because her hole was seeming to be closing by itself. Three months later, she started leaking out her hole and it should've been closed.

So, the doctors decided to give Lay stitches in order to close the hole correctly, and after that everything started going normal with our life. Earlier she was having problems with her weight, it still wasn't how it was supposed to be. The GI doctor changed her formula again to elecare Jr. this formula came with different flavors (unflavored, chocolate, vanilla and bananas). Her favorite kind was vanilla, this type of baby milk wasn't on the shelfs like the others. I had to order them by the pharmacy. This milk has the nutrition she really needed to help her gain weight faster. She had to drink that every 4-6 times a day. I hate giving it to her, she always coughs when she drinks that milk. I'm not sure if it was because the scoops the doctor told us but I cutted back. I sooner later took her off it because I felt like she got a little older and didn't need it. Had to put her back on the milk due to her weight again but the doctor told me to do it only once a day. They gave me some medicine this time so she would not cough when she drank it. Lay going be under doctor order for a minute.

Lay started crawling, talking, walking, and getting into everything. After things were getting better, her doctors referred her to therapy. I did some extensive research and decided to try the Baby Can't Wait program. With this program a therapist comes to your child's school or home, once a week. To work on things such as speech and interactions. The first therapist that came once a week to see her, Lay seemed to not like the therapist at all. I left her alone a few times to see if she was going to be better if I'm out of sight, but I always went back up because she would continue to do the screaming. So, eventually I stopped leaving, stayed during the sessions and interacted with Lay and her therapist.

After a few more sessions, Lay moved up to physical therapy, and received a different therapist. Physical therapy was needed for Lay because when she walked her legs would start bending, and The Therapist suggested for her father and myself to get her into braces for her legs so she could stand up straight. I didn't want any problems down the road, so I told the therapist that we would try it. Even though I really didn't want to do it because I felt that she would get better with time, we still attempted the leg brace.

We barely saw Lay's physical therapist due to scheduling conflict, so I was doing work with her myself. I suggested that her father work with her as well, but he was too afraid of hurting her or making things worse. So, we only were in it for two months and eventually it stopped. Everything was looking good, but my only concern was her speech. So, we did a checkup with the Baby Can't Wait director and I told her about wanting to get speech therapy because I want to get everything for my girl while I can.

The Baby Can't Wait Director set up a meeting with a lady to come to look at Lay to see if speech therapy is necessary. They agreed Lay needed therapy, so the Speech therapist came every week. Lay loves that therapist so much and every time the therapist would come, she would know it's time to learn. She started doing well with making sounds, pronouncing words, as well as picking out and saying what she wants. And now Lay is finally catching up, even though she was born preemie, she's smart. Looking at her I share a tear, because my baby girl is growing up. She has come so far and our God Never gave up on her. I remember we were watching her grow out the wound and now into a big girl. God is good. If you never believed God, you better do that now.

Life went good just how we imagined. Holidays were spent together, birthday went a little bitter, we even brought in the new year as a family, the right way. Family is very important to me and I pray we continue to stay strong and God will keep us to raise our daughter together. As time moving, we started potty training her, with the goal of being fully potty trained by three. Lay has her days like many children but Lay also knows how to go to the potty she just chooses not to. Lay knows when she uses her potty, to call whoever around her to show she did it and clap her hands afterwards.

One morning we got up to use the restroom, and Lay didn't want to use it at that moment, so I told her if she uses the bathroom on herself that I was going to discipline her. She understood, and we both went into the living room. While Lay played in the living room I tucked my head into my phone, a couple minutes had pass and I didn't notice lay had went the back of the house to use the restroom, so when she came running back she kept saying "mama, mama, peepee". So I went on the back of the house and she told me look, because Ca'Layia use it in her potty. I was so excited, I shed a tear because she's growing up, but I wish she could stay a baby.

As a parent you don't know what you are going to get out of the child. She has a big personality so I often don't know what she would do, because now we call her name and tell her to stop every second of the day. She's not a people person and will look at you crazy, but I just love it now we are all together, it's the day we've been waiting for. We are a blessed family and we are going to always stick together.

This journey was scary, you don't know how things are going to turn out. Some people ask me how could you do that? I probably would've given up. It is about having faith in the man above. It was very hard for me but I tried my hardest. I prayed so much I believe God had me at the end. Once again it was hard trusting him. My cousin and I were in the situation of having our child early due to preeclampsia. Instead she had her baby girl the month after me. She had her baby girl 27 weeks, and wasn't long enough she went home. One day I actually was sitting down in my thoughts. I know you can't question God I started doubting. I had my baby first and she was in the NICU still.

WHY? I started crying because it wasn't right that she was still in there. Lay godmother encouraged me, I felt a lot better. Just hold on and keep the faith. It was hard, nobody knew what I was going through on the inside. I always smile on the outside for not letting everything bother me. I listen to gospel to get my mind off this. I remember my grandmother/ mother told me to always give God his time because one he is going but you in a situation that you not don't have any choice but to go to him. My mom was my peace maker when she was around. I felt like everything is good. I had to snap back and think I had been through alot before having my daughter. God didn't let me down. I just started trusting him and stayed positive. Sometimes I thought about babies having more issues than my child. It could've been worse but God. There are babies who are born earlier than 26 weeks, have been in the NICU longer than her, and have worse problems than my child. I thanked God for not letting me down and blessing my family.

Can you walk in the mother's shoes? When her baby had to get brain and heart surgery. You have children fight for their life every day. But as parents we don't give up on our children, they need us the most, but we need them too. Nobody knows how to love them. When the doctor told me how things were going to end up with my daughter, God turned all the way around. My daughter is not taking medicine on a daily basis, she doesn't need help with walking, eating and everyday she is learning new words.

We don't know what God's plans are but just trust him and stand on his word. He will not fail you and will not put more on you can bare. I had my moments in not having faith nobody because I was praying so much nothing seemed like it was happening. But you gotta wait for our time, not God's time just to keep faith.

It's just scary because we don't know the outcome but still to have the mustard of faith. I remember in the NICU I had experienced a baby whose heart rate was dropping low. As I saw doctors and nurses running in the room, I said a prayer for the baby and called my mom to tell her what happened and to also say a prayer. I'm not 100% spiritual but my mom is. Roughly five to ten minutes later the baby boy heart rate started coming up. Pregnancy can be scary, you never know what's gonna happen. All you got to pray. People have kids and don't want to give it. Why? Some people are not ready to have kids or can't take care of them. That's not an excuse because we have protection out here. I snuggle to put it up for an apportion let that child be a blessing to someone else. It's women out here who can't have kids. Kids are a blessing I wish I went a full 9 months but God had other plans. I was scared for my life but kept the faith.

Everybody is scared to lose a child and some mothers have done it and it feels like the end of the world. Yes, it's hard to get over that type of heartbreak that's the worst heartbreak--losing a child. A child you see every day, you get up in the middle of night to change or feed, a child who calls your name, a child who brings so much joy and makes you go harder. I wouldn't want myself or anybody to go through that heartbreak. You can't see that child anymore and it's hurtful. But just know don't give up on life and go harder just like the child is here. Even full-term babies can have problems. You never know how your pregnancy will turn out, but just pray it comes out good.

All babies are miracles and mothers are blessings because pregnancy is scary. Babies enter the NICU life with different problems but as time comes along things start getting better for the babies and the mothers must balance out their outside life and NICU life together. Some mothers must work, and some stay home for a few months, but at work you're not around your child therefore, your child is constantly on your mind all day. If you have other kids at home, you must make sure they're good and still make time to go see your child in the NICU While I was at work my mother and/or sister would check on Lay while she's in the NICU, and after work I still went and stayed for hours.

Sometimes you don't really have time for yourself dealing with the NICU. Could you deal with this? Some mothers have complications in their pregnancy and so for the safety of the baby the mother there's no choice but for the baby to be born early. Sometimes the mother can even pass away, and the child is left without a mother or vice versa. If you must choose who will you want to save your child or yourself? Personally, I wouldn't want to choose, because I don't want anyone else to raise my child, but at the same time I could have another; But if they can save both of us it will be a blessing. Let's enjoy our life with them, because hey they didn't ask to be here! Out of my hold lift I never thought how pregnancy can be so scary. Having a child wasn't really something I thought of really. I told myself I wanted to have a child before I hit 30. Why didn't I get on birth control? The first time I got on the pills but that didn't work out, the second time I was scared to try stuff new.

I see birth control infect people in many ways and I loved my body so I didn't want any change. But I wasn't getting pregnant back to back. I was scared. After this journey I got on birth control right away. Am I gonna have another kid in the future? I say I want another one, but I'm scared. I almost lost my life with Lay. I didn't want to leave my baby in this world without a mother she never met. I love my child so much. I cherish every moment with this little girl. I might just give her a sister or brother one day in the future. Right now I'm focused on us. When I have another child I want to be in place hopefully have a ring on my finger. My child's father and I are still together. Some mothers are not in their child life and I'm not the one to judge but your kid/kids need you! If you have kids in this world, give them that time and show them that love. It's not all about buying, it's giving them that mother and father's attention. Don't let them go find it in the wrong place. Who doesn't want to see the child/children grow up and be something in life. Mothers get overwhelmed and need a break. A mother's job is never done. The child/children need this and that. Plus worrying about the problems we have going on. It gets depressing at times we still get to smile when you act like things are okay. But look at your child/children everything will be okay. After all my child went though I look at her everyday and thank God. I'll tell her somedays to say thank you to God. She is a walking miracle. Forever bless, she will not fail. Kids are our motative, let's go hard for them.

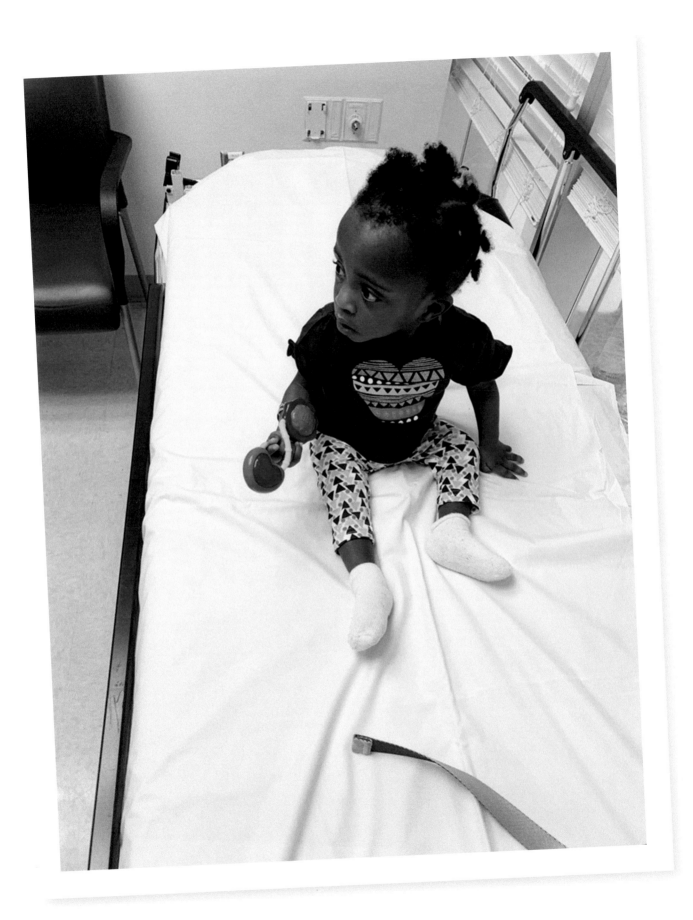

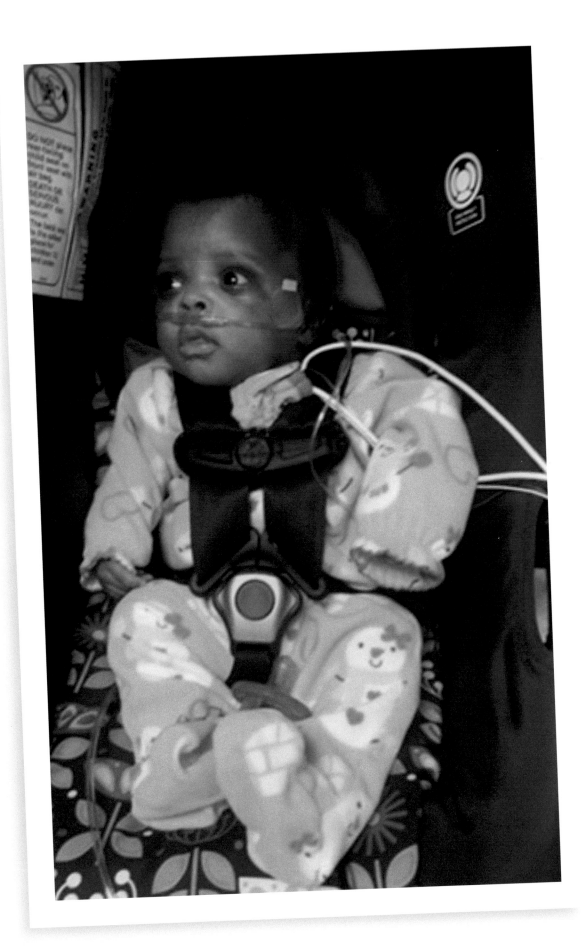

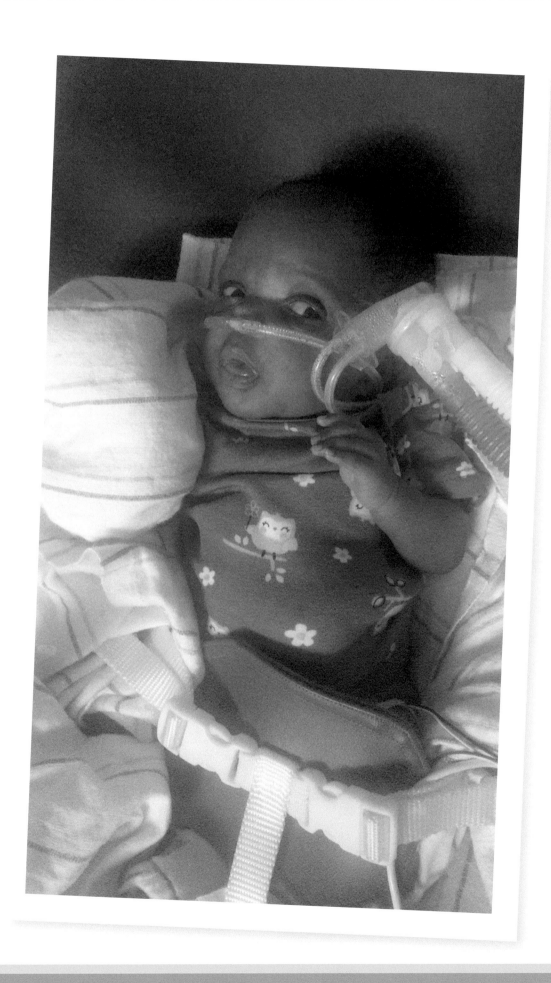

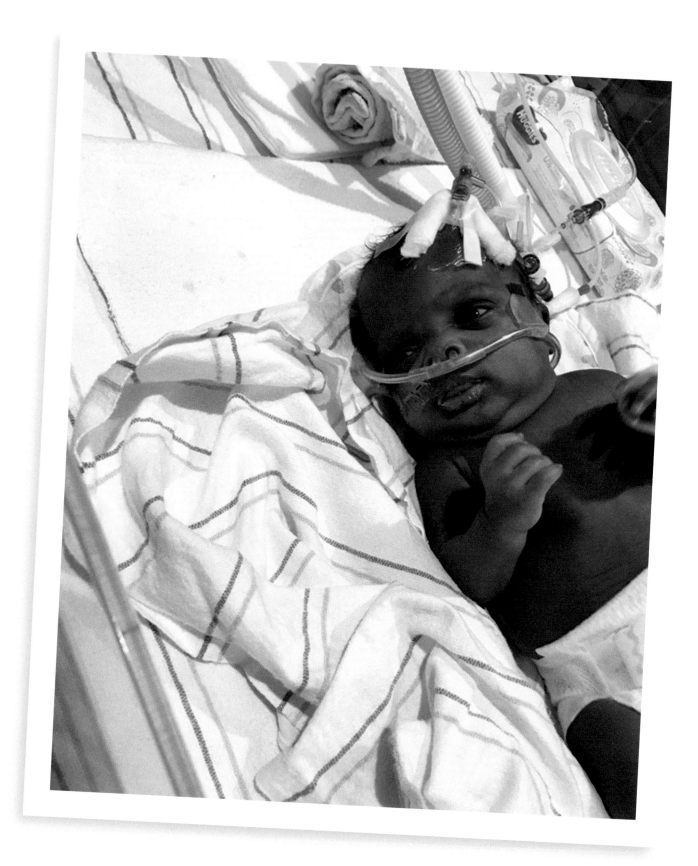

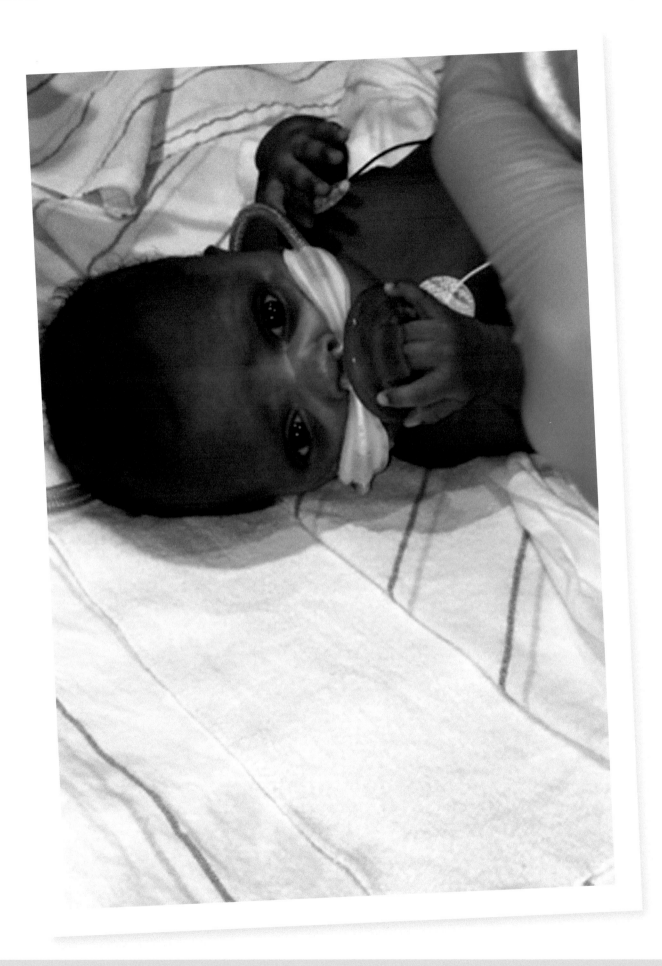

Printed in the United States
By Bookmasters